Elizabeth Buffum Chace

Anti-Slavery Reminiscences

Elizabeth Buffum Chace

Anti-Slavery Reminiscences

ISBN/EAN: 9783744732840

Printed in Europe, USA, Canada, Australia, Japan

Cover: Foto ©ninafisch / pixelio.de

More available books at **www.hansebooks.com**

ANTI-SLAVERY

REMINISCENCES.

ELIZABETH BUFFUM CHACE.

CENTRAL FALLS, R. I.
E. L. FREEMAN & SON, STATE PRINTERS.
1891.

TO MY

Beloved Son and Daughters,

I DEDICATE THIS RECORD OF A PORTION OF MY LIFE,

IN THE REMEMBRANCE OF WHICH,

AMONG MANY FAILURES AND SHORT-COMINGS,

I NOW, IN THE

EIGHTY-FIFTH YEAR OF MY AGE,

FIND THE MOST ENTIRE SATISFACTION,

AND I HOPE THAT THEY AND THEIR CHILDREN

MAY GATHER THEREFROM

SOME LESSONS OF

ADHERENCE TO PRINCIPLE AND DEVOTION TO DUTY,

AT WHATEVER COST

OF WORLDLY PROSPERITY OR ADVANCEMENT.

ANTI-SLAVERY REMINISCENCES.

M Y Anti Slavery reminiscences date back to a
very early period in my life. My maternal
ancestor, Daniel Gould, came from England, and
settled in Newport, Rhode Island, in the year
1637. He became a member of the Society of
Friends, commonly called Quakers; and, marry-
ing the daughter of John Coggeshall, the first
President of the Aquidneck Colony, who was also
a Quaker, the descendants of the two families,
for many generations, must have constituted a
large portion of the society of Friends there—the
first date of the existence of said society, in its
original Book of Discipline, being 1675. The town
of Newport became a slave market; and I have rea-
son to believe that these Quaker ancestors of mine,
in common with other commercial citizens of that
seaport, were somewhat implicated in the African

slave trade. But, the spirit of early Quakerism could not wholly sanction this terrible iniquity; and so, as early as 1727 the yearly meeting began to issue advices and remonstrances against it: the first recorded being as follows: "It is the sense of this meeting, that the importation of Negroes from their native country is not a commendable practice, and that practice is censured by this meeting." In 1760 the yearly meeting issued another advice to Friends "to keep their hands clear of this unrighteous gain of oppression," and yet without absolute prohibition. In 1773, "It is recommended to Friends, who have slaves in possession, to treat them with tenderness, impress God's fear in their minds, promote their attending places of religious worship, and give those who are young, at least, so much learning that they may be capable of reading." The same year, they also advise that "the young, and also the aged and impotent, be set free." The last record in the Book of Discipline is dated 1780, and disposes of the matter thus: "Agreed, that no friend import, or any ways purchase, dispose of, or hold mankind as slaves; but, that all those who have been held in a state of slavery, be discharged therefrom; that all those be used well who are under friends' care, and are not in circumstances, through non-age or incapacity, to minister to their own necessities; and that they give to those who are young, such an education as becomes Christians, and encourage others in a religious and virtuous life." Thus, the New England Yearly Meeting, held in Newport, Rhode Island, abolished slavery among its members, in the year 1780, while it was still legalized by the New England States.

My grandmother, Sarah Gould, was born near the year 1737, and her father, James Coggeshall, soon after her birth, purchased a little African girl, from a slave-ship just come into port, to serve as nurse-maid to the child. She remained a slave in the household, until the Friends abolished slavery among themselves in 1780, when, becoming a free woman, she established herself as a cake-maker and confectioner in the town, and lived esteemed and respected to a very old age. In my very infancy, my mother used to tell to my sisters and myself, the story of this girl, Morier, who was stolen from her home and brought up a slave in our great-grandfather's house; and of the strength of her attachment to our grandmother, whom she nursed

in infancy.   My mother remembered, as a child,
her frequent visits to the homestead, and the affec-
tionate welcome which always greeted her there.
But, in all this story, which made a strong impres-
sion on our minds, our gentle mother gave us no
idea that she thought it was ever right to buy little
girls and hold them as slaves, although it was done
by her own grandfather; so that we never had any
predilections in favor of slavery.

My paternal grandfather, William Buffum, of
Smithfield, also a Quaker, was a member of the
Rhode Island Society for the gradual abolition of
slavery; which was probably organized near the
time when slavery was abolished in the State.

When my father, Arnold Buffum, was a child, it
was not uncommon for fugitive slaves from New
York, to seek refuge in Rhode Island; although the
United States Constitution guaranteed to the slave-
holder, the right to recapture them in any part of
the country.   On one occasion, a whole family who
had escaped, and been for some months in hiding,
came to my grandfather's house.   They were established in a farm house near the homestead, and
employment was furnished to the father and the
older children.   In a short time, their place of

refuge was discovered, and one day, the slave-master from New York, accompanied by an officer, came riding up from Providence to arrest them. The neighbors were hastily summoned, and with the household of my grandfather, formed a human barricade, opposed to their entrance through the gates. A smart young colored laborer, who had become attached to one of the fugitive's daughters, brandished a knife before the slave catchers, and threatened to "pudding" them, if they did not depart; and the calm determination, with, perhaps, some wiser threats of the assembled and constantly increasing company of defenders, succeeded in driving them away without their prey: and the family remained without further molestation. In my childhood, my father used to tell us how, as a little boy, he stood between Pedro's knees, and listened to his tales of the sufferings of the slaves, of their capture in Africa, the miseries of the slave-ship, and of his own adventures in the escape with his family; the fond father ending by placing his hand on the curly head of his youngest child, and exclaiming, "And Pedro love Cuffie better than all his chillen, cause he be free born." And so, my father became an abolitionist in his childhood; and his detestatation of the "sum of all villanies," grew with his growth and strengthened with his strength, and never weakened or wavered throughout his long life. I think when the Colonization Society was formed, he gave in his adhesion to that, in the belief, shared by many other good men, that this was the way out of the terrible evil. When Benjamin Lundy came with his appeals for gradual abolition, he hoped for rescue by this means, but, when William Lloyd Garrison raised the cry for "immediate and unconditional emancipation," my father's clear head, his tender heart, and his unshrinking conscience, embraced, without doubt or question, the principles of the Garrisonian Anti-Slavery movement. He became the first President of the New England Anti-Slavery Society, and lived and labored in and for the cause for many years, though obloquy and persecution pursued and assailed him therefor. Thus was I born and baptized into the Anti-Slavery spirit. Our family were all Abolitionists.

Never, in our large household, do I recall one word short of condemnation of the vile system. In our minds there were no palliating circumstances. The slave-holders were man-stealers; and, as one of the earliest of the lecturers used constantly to de-

clare, they must " quit stealing." When I married,
and my husband's attention was called to the question, he readily accepted the Anti-Slavery principles, and remained faithful thereto, during his life.

Up to the time of the issue of the first number of
the *Liberator*, in the year 1831, we had believed there
should be devised some scheme for gradual emancipation, as did our father. Soon after that, when he
came to my home at Fall River, and brought us the
new paper, and told us of having met Garrison and
heard his arguments, and how the New England Society had been formed, I remember asking him if he
thought it would be quite safe to set the slaves free all
at once. In a few words, he dispelled, once for all,
that illusion from my mind; and from that hour we
were all Garrisonians. I remember well, how
eager we were, in our revived Anti-Slavery zeal, to
present the cause of the slave to everybody we met;
not doubting that, when their attention was called
to it, they would be ready, as we were, to demand
his immediate emancipation. But, alas! their commercial relations, their political associations, and
with many, their religious fellowship with the people of the South, so blinded the eyes, hardened the
hearts and stifled the consciences of the North, that

we found very few people who were ready to give
any countenance or support to the new Anti-
Slavery movement.

My father and mother were, by inheritance, by
education and by conviction, members of the
Society of Friends: and were devoted to its principles, its service and mode of worship; and their
children, being also birth-right members, had been
taught great reverence and respect for its ministers
and elders, as well as for all the doctrines and
peculiar customs of the Society. The idea of
infallibility, without using the word, was at that
time, strong in the family mind. So, from the
Friends surely, we expected sympathy and co-
operation. But, as we met them, individually or
in groups, and made our appeal for the slave, we
were shocked to find that even they, whose fore-
fathers had abolished slavery among themselves,
while it was still legalized by the State, and had
inserted in their Book of Discipline, the advice to
be often read, "That Friends be careful to maintain
our testimony faithfully against slavery," had become so demoralized, that they too, with rare ex-
ceptions, shut their eyes to the great iniquity.
They objected to the strong, denunciatory language

of the *Liberator*; they disapproved of Friends uniting with other people in public meetings or in philanthropic work; they did not think the slaves should be set free all at once, and they did not want their daughters to marry negroes. I remember making an appeal to a Quaker brother-in-law of mine, by asking him if he did not think the slaves should be freed, and his only reply was, "I shouldn't want to see a black man sitting on the sofa beside my daughter."

We went to our yearly meeting at Newport, and there, slavery was the chief topic of conversation, at the hotel where many Friends were staying; so stirred were people everywhere, either for or against the system, by the new awakening. But almost everybody was against us. They denounced the *Liberator*; Garrison was an infidel; slavery could only be cut off gradually; the colored race must be colonized in Africa. Joseph Bowne, a distinguished preacher from New York, was heard to declare, that, if he could set all the slaves free, within thirty years, by turning over his hand, he would not do it. In the meeting, we were cautioned by our ministers, not to give way to excitement, but to keep in the quiet, and wait for Divine guidance; and not to unite with people outside of our religious society, in public undertakings. Those who had already made themselves obnoxious in these ways, were ignored in the appointment of committees; and some who stood on standing committees, were dropped therefrom. There was a general treatment of such as were known to be Abolitionists, as suspicious persons—persons to be overlooked and avoided.

I had, from my childhood, been a devout believer in and defender of orthodox Quakerism. I had been Overseer of the Poor, in Swanzey monthly meeting, its assistant clerk, and finally its clerk; and had been, in various ways, "made use of," as the phrase was in the Society. I wore the Quaker costume in its entirety, and had never said "you" to a single person in my life, or given the title of "Mr." or "Mrs." to anybody. I was constant in the attendance of our religious meetings, and firmly believed in the efficacy of our simple, and as we called them, unceremonious modes of worship. But, to be an Abolitionist, put me down among the ostracized. I remember, on one occasion, at the yearly meeting, when an epistle, prepared to be sent to a distant yearly meeting, was read by the clerk and presented for approval, which contained the usual formula of the declaration of our testimony against the enslavement of "Africans," I objected to this designation, as most of the slaves in this country, at that time, were natives of America. Another Anti-Slavery woman seconded my remonstrance, and finally the word was changed. We afterward learned, that a friend present from Philadelphia, inquired *who those young women vere*, and expressed her surprise that our protest was heeded, " as such a proposal coming from a person *in the body of the house*. would be entirely unnoticed in Philadelphia yearly meeting."

At that time, the prejudice against color, throughout New England, was even stronger than the pro-slavery spirit. On one occasion, my husband and myself went to Boston, to attend the annual meeting of the New England Anti-Slavery Society. Accompanied by a gentleman friend, we drove to Taunton from Fall River, there to take the railroad, which I think, at that time, furnished only one car for the journey. As we entered the car, Samuel Rodman, an Anti-Slavery man from New Bedford, and a highly respectable, well-dressed colored man and his wife, from the same town, took seats therein also. The conductor came and ordered the colored people to leave the car. We all remonstrated, of course, but without avail. He called the superintendent, who peremptorily repeated the order. They got out quietly, and we did the same, (but not so quietly,) and retired to the waiting-room, leaving the car empty. The officials held a conference outside, and the conductor soon informed us that an extra car had been put on for the negroes, and invited us to take the seats we had left. We held a little conference among ourselves, and then every one of us entered the car with the colored people. The superintendent was very angry, but he did not quite dare to order us out, so he assured us that our conduct would avail nothing, for no negroes would ever be permitted to be mixed up with white people on that road. They were mixed up with us, however, on that day, and we found them intelligent, agreeable companions.

In some cases, persons who were opposed to slavery and were willing to work for its abolition, still strongly objected to any association with colored persons in their Anti-Slavery labors. We organized a Female Anti-Slavery Society at Fall River, about the year 1835. In the village were a few very respectable young colored women, who came to our meetings. One evening, soon after the Society was formed, my sister and myself went to them and invited them to join. This raised such a storm among some of the leading members, that for a time, it threatened the dissolution of the Society. They said they had no objection to these women attending the meetings, and they were willing to help and encourage them in every way, but they did not think it was at all proper to invite them to join the Society, thus putting them on an equality with ourselves. We maintained our ground, however, and the colored women were admitted.*

At one time, when we had an Anti-Slavery Convention at Fall River, a large number of visitors dined at our house. Among them were the two New Bedford people, who had so shocked the sensi-

* I regret to be obliged, as a faithful chronicler of my Anti-Slavery experiences, to state, that in the year 1877, twelve years after the abolition of slavery, and many more years after the admission of colored children into the public schools of the city of Providence, my daughters and myself were compelled, conscientiously, to resign our membership in the Rhode Island Women's Club, because that body refused admission to a highly respectable, well-educated woman, solely on account of the color of her skin, although she had been a teacher of a colored school in that city for twenty-five years.

2

bilities of the railroad officials at Taunton, and, I think, Charles Lenox Remoud, a young colored Anti-Slavery orator. We had then in our house, in some useful capacity, a devoted Baptist woman, who usually sat at the family table. When the dinner was ready, I asked her to come. She replied, " No ; I don't eat with niggers." When the dinner was over and the guests had retired to the parlor, I called her again. And again she answered, " No : I don't eat *with* niggers nor *after* 'em." Whether she went hungry that day, I never inquired.

In the year 1839, my husband and myself removed with our family to Valley Falls, Rhode Island, bringing our Anti-Slavery principles with us. And, though he had been a consistent Friend from his youth up, and I remained clerk of Swanzey monthly meeting, until obliged to resign on account of our removal, the certificate they gave us to Providence monthly meeting, was deficient in respect to our standing, in that it omitted the usual acknowledgment that we were " of orderly lives and conversation," and only declared our membership in the Society.

Our Anti-Slavery attitude soon put us under the ban of disapproval among Providence Friends.

One day, soon after our removal, I was walking on the street in the city, when the leading minister of Providence monthly meeting, overtook me, and greeted me very cordially. Walking beside me, he told me that he and his wife, (also a minister,) intended to call on us soon. I assured him of a hearty welcome. And then I remembered that I had in my pocket, an address to American Friends, on their inconsistent attitude toward the slavery question, by Joseph Sturge, an eminent English Friend, who had recently travelled in this country, and who had been an active laborer in the Anti-Slavery cause at home. I asked the friend if he had seen it, and he said he had not, and I gave him the copy I had with me. His manner toward me changed at once, and he soon left me, and the proposed call from himself and his wife was never made.

Within a few years following our removal to Rhode Island, many occurrences took place, which proved that the Society of Friends in this country, was forgetful of its earlier record, and, like the other churches, had submitted to the domination of the slave-holding power. Uxbridge monthly meeting disowned Abby Kelley for Anti-Slavery lecturing, although they did so, ostensibly, on some frivolous charges, which had no real foundation in fact. Smithfield monthly meeting disowned my father, on charges which he proved to them were false, and when he did so, and remonstrated against their threatened action, he was assured by the leading authority in the meeting, that it could "all be amicably settled, if he would give up this abolition lecturing," thus admitting that this was the offence for which he was to be disowned. Several persons, in various parts of the country, were forcibly carried out of Friends' meetings, for attempting therein to urge upon friends the duty " to maintain faithfully their testimony against slavery," as their Discipline required. A few meeting houses in country places, had been opened for Anti-Slavery meetings: whereupon, our New England Yearly Meeting adopted a rule, that no meeting house, under its jurisdiction, should be opened, except for the meetings of our religious Society.

During those years, I could not help feeling a sense of grave responsibility for these unrighteous proceedings, so long as I remained a member of the Society, and my mind was deeply exercised concerning my duty in the matter. Other Anti-Slavery

friends thought it was best to remain in the Society,
and strive to reform these abuses. But, we were
few in number; and the great body of Quakerism
in the country was against us. Our lips were
sealed in the meetings, and, out of meetings, we
were in disgrace—"despised and rejected." One
young Friend in Massachusetts, had written a very
earnest, open letter to Friends, in remonstrance for
their pro-slavery position. He was universally
condemned by all the powerful influences of the
Society. Talking with one of the most influential
members of our Yearly Meeting, who expressed
strong condemnation of this young man's presump-
tion, I said, " But is not what he says, true?" And
he replied, " Well, thee may be sure, it will cer-
tainly kill him as a Friend."

No belief in Papal infallibility, was ever stronger
in the Catholic mind, than was the assumption
(not expressed in words) that the Society could do
no wrong; and that, on this question of slavery,
silence should be maintained; and no reproof, ex-
hortation or entreaty against the pro-slavery attitude of the Society, should be tolerated. The claim
of Friends, that the transaction of their Society
affairs, should be under the immediate inspiration

and guidance of the Holy Spirit, so beautifully set forth in many of their writings and sermons, as well as required in their Discipline, was sometimes perverted, to authorize proceedings and actions which were far from being holy.

Finally, after a long struggle, I was compelled, in order to secure my own peace of mind, to resign my membership in the Society, to which, from my childhood, I had been most devoutly attached. My husband remained in the meeting, and the separation between the Wilburites and the Gurney-ites, soon occurring, he retired with the former, and preserved, through the remainder of his life, unmo-lested and respected, his Anti-Slavery character; while I lost what little caste I held among the Friends, many of whom were near and dear to me by kin, and some of them by the nearer and dearer ties of life-long association and friendship. But, with my family cares and labor for the cause of the slave, and the associations it brought me, I had no time or inclination to worry over lost friendships; and the relief from responsibility for the pro-slavery attitude of the Society, was sufficient compensation for all I thus relinquished.

Before leaving Fall River, we had a very interest-

ing experience with a fugitive slave, named James
Curry, an intelligent young man from North Caro-
lina, whose thrilling story I had narrated in the
columns of the *Liberator* of January 10. 1840.
After coming to Rhode Island, our house became
the resting place for the advocates of freedom for the
slave, when travelling, or lecturing in this region,
until the fetters which bound him were broken.
William Lloyd Garrison, Wendell Phillips, Parker
Pillsbury, Stephen S. Foster, Abby Kelley, Henry
C. Wright, Charles Remond, Frederick Douglass,
Charles and Cyrus Burleigh, Lucy Stone, William
Wells Brown and others of less note, were often our
guests ; and our children were born and bred in the
atmosphere which these lovers of freedom helped to
create in our household. The career of all these
men and women should be written for the perusal
of coming generations, as grand examples of noble,
self-sacrificing manhood and womanhood, such as
the world has seldom proved itself capable of pro-
ducing. When my own dear father and mother
were with us, as they often were, through their
serene old age, the condemnation of slavery and
the praises of liberty were always upon his lips.
I can now seem to hear his rich, mellow voice,

as he strolled about the house, reciting in the sing-song Quaker fashion, the lines of Cowper—

> " I would not have a slave to till my ground,
> To carry me, to fan me while I sleep,
> And tremble when I wake, for all the gold
> That sinews bought and sold have ever earned.
> No; dear as freedom is, and, in my heart's
> Just estimation, prized above all price,
> I would much rather be myself the slave,
> And wear the bonds, than fasten them on him;"

or Montgomery's, on the Abolition of the Slave-trade by Great Britain——

> " Thy chains are broken, Africa, be free!"
> Thus saith the Island-empress of the sea;
> Thus saith Britannia, O, ye winds and waves!
> Waft the glad tidings to the land of slaves.
> Proclaim on Guinea's coast, by Gambia's side,
> And far as Niger rolls his eastern tide,
> Through radiant realms, beneath the burning zone,
> Where Europe's curse is felt, her name unknown,
> Thus saith Britannia, empress of the sea,
> " Thy chains are broken, Africa, be free!"

And, other quotations of similar character. The songs of freedom from our young poet Whittier, then being issued from the press, my father was too old to commit to his already well-stored memory.

The *Liberator* and the Anti Slavery *Standard* were

our favorite newspapers ; and Uncle Tom's Cabin,
The White Slave, and other books of like purpose,
were preferred before all others ; while they shared
with Robinson Crusoe, the Swiss Family Robinson,
and other story books, the ordinary reading of our
children, in their very early years.

As the Anti-Slavery agitation had created
throughout the Northern States, an ever increasing sentiment against the iniquitous system, it
could not fail to produce some effect on the South,
occasionally of sympathy, but usually of bitter
animosity, which was continually calling for the
adoption of more stringent measures against Northern influence and interference. Travellers from
the North, were subjected to the most rigid es-
pionage, and sometimes, to personal indignity ;
one pious young man, selling Cottage Bibles, in
Nashville, Tennessee, being publicly whipped, because, his wagon being searched, one copy of the
book was found to be wrapped in a copy of the
Liberator. A reward of $5000, was offered, by the
State of Georgia, for the body of Mr. Garrison ; and
it became entirely unsafe for any person who could
not prove himself to be in favor of slavery, to
travel in any State farther south than Pennsyl-

vania and New Jersey. The slaves themselves,
caught more and more, the excitement of the agitation: and consequently, the number of escapes
increased, from year to year.

Although the holding of human beings in the
Southern States, as slaves, and the right to recapture them in any part of the United States, were
guaranteed by our National Constitution, it was
found to be insufficient, inasmuch as it did not
make resistance to their capture, sufficiently penal.
So, at the bidding of the slave-holding power, the
famous fugitive slave law was enacted by the Congress of 1850: Daniel Webster strongly defending
its adoption, on the 7th of March, in a speech in
the United States Senate, which has made his name
infamous, in the reformed sentiment of New England.

Still, the Anti-Slavery spirit grew and prospered,
in proportion to the increase of the difficulties in
its way. All through the States on the border line,
were friends, who, in spite of the law, and the pro-
slavery spirit around them, were ever ready to con-
ceal, protect, and succor the fugitive, until he
could be sent to the British Dominion, where the
slave-master could not reach him. Many were

caught and returned to slavery, with all its horrors ; still, one way and another, there were a good many who did reach Canada, and thus escape the vigilance of the mercenary human blood hounds, who, as United States officers, were ever on the watch to make them their prey.

From the time of the arrival of James Curry at Fall River, and his departure for Canada, in 1839, that town became an important station, on the so-called underground railroad. Slaves in Virginia, would secure passage, either secretly or with consent of the Captains, in small trading vessels, at Norfolk or Portsmouth, and thus be brought into some port in New England, where their fate depended on the circumstances into which they happened to fall. A few, landing in some town on Cape Cod, would reach New Bedford, and thence be sent by an abolitionist there to Fall River, to be sheltered by Nathaniel B. Borden and his wife, who was my sister Sarah, and sent by them, to Valley Falls, in the darkness of night, and in a closed carriage, with Robert Adams, a most faithful friend, as their conductor. Here, we received them, and, after preparing them for the journey, my husband would accompany them a short distance,

on the Providence and Worcester railroad, acquaint
the conductor with the facts, enlist his interest in
their behalf, and then leave them in his care, to be
transferred at Worcester, to the Vermont road, from
which, by a previous general arrangement, they
were received by a Unitarian clergyman named
Young, and sent by him to Canada, where they
uniformly arrived safely. I used to give them an
envelope, directed to us, to be mailed in Toronto,
which, when it reached us, was sufficient by its
post-mark, to announce their safe arrival, beyond
the baleful influence of the Stars and Stripes, and
the anti-protection of the fugitive slave law.

One evening, in answer to the summons at our
door, we were met by Mr. Adams and a person,
apparently in a woman's Quaker costume, whose
face was concealed by a thick veil. The person,
however, proved to be a large, noble-looking colored man, whose story was soon told. He had
escaped from Virginia, bringing away with him a
wife and child. Reaching New Bedford, he had
found employment, which he had quietly pursued,
for eleven months. Being a very valuable piece of
property, (I think he was a blacksmith), his master
had spared no pains in discovering his whereabouts;

and, finally, traced him to New Bedford. Coming
to Boston, he secured the services of a constable,
and repaired to New Bedford, and went prowling
round in search of his victim. But, the colored
people of that town, discovered their purpose, com-
municated with some of the few abolitionists, and
the man was hurried off to Fall River, before
the man-stealers had time to find him ; and the
Friends there, dressed him in Quaker bonnet and
shawl, and sent him off in the daylight, not daring
to keep him till night, lest his master should follow
immediately. He said he carried a revolver in his
pocket, and, if his master should overtake him on
the road, he would defend himself to the death of
one of them, for, no slave would he ever be again.
We sent him off on the early morning train, with
fear and trembling ; but, had the happiness in a
few days, to learn of his safe arrival, of his having
procured work, at once ; and, afterwards, that he
had been joined by his wife and child. His master,
after searching for him a whole day, in New Bedford, had returned to Boston, very much disgusted
with the indifference of the " Yankee Mudsills,"
(as the lordly Southerners used to call New Eng-
landers), to the misfortunes of the slave-holders ;

and wrote an indignant letter to a Boston pro-slavery newspaper, in which he complained bitterly of their want of sympathy and co-operation, in his endeavor to recover his property. He said that, when he arrived in New Bedford, the bells were rung, to announce his coming, and warn his slave, thus aiding in his escape; and that, every way, he was badly treated. The truth was, as we afterward learned, that he arrived at nine o'clock in the morning, just as the school-bells were ringing; and he understood this as a personal indignity.

Another time, we were aroused about midnight, by the arrival of the good friend Adams, with two young men, about twenty-four years old. They also were from Portsmouth, Virginia. They had each secured a passage on a small trading vessel, bound to Wareham, Massachusetts, through the friendly interest of the colored steward, but without the knowledge of each other, or of the Captain and crew of the vessel; and they were strangers to one another before their escape. The steward concealed one in the hold, and the other in his own berth, in the little cabin he had all to himself, and he carried them food in the night. They belonged to different masters, and had each a wife and child.

whom they said they would never have left, had they not learned that they were soon to be separated from them, and sold to the far South. So cruel was slavery in this country, less than forty years ago! They were three days on the voyage. Before their arrival, the steward told them of the presence of each other, and, as they would reach the port in the night, he requested them to remain concealed, until three o'clock the next afternoon, at which time, he should have left the vessel, as he should not engage for a return voyage. Then he instructed them how to proceed when they reached the shore. The rest of the story I will give as nearly as I can, in the words of the man who occupied the steward's berth, premising, that it was then a time of extreme cold weather, about the last of February; the ground being covered with ice and snow, and everything in a freezing condition.

"I was lyin' in de berth, while dey was unloadin' de cargo, an' I heered some one comin' toward de place where I lay. Dere had ben a leak in de vessel, an' de Cap'n, he was searchin' round tryin' to find it. I covered myself wid de bedcloes, and flattened myself out like a plank, so I couldn't be seen. He come an' reached over me, feelin' along de side o' de vessel for de leak, and, as he drew back his hand, it hit my head ; an' den he stripped off de cloes, an' dere I lay. Oh! den, I fell to beggin' an' prayin' him to let me go, but he went out widout speakin' a word, an' I heered him bolt two doors between me an' de deck. He meant to carry me back ; but, God knows I couldn't go back dere no more, an' I alongside o' dat wharf. My coat, an' my hat, an' my shoes, was under dat berth, but I didn't stop for dem ; and I bust open de two doors, reached de deck, an' jumped on de wharf, before dey had time to stop me. De Cap'n, he called to de men to seize me, but dey never moved ; an' I run up de street as fast as I could. I found de colored woman and her son, de steward tole me to go to, an' dey took me in, an' de neighbors come in: an' dey warmed me, an' fed me, an' put cloes on me, an' I don' know what dey didn't do to me."

Then the poor, brave fellow told them there was another fugitive on board the vessel. And an old white man said he knew the Captain, and he would go down and get him off. So, he went ; it was dark, and he succeeded in finding the man in the hold, and brought him away without discovery; and the Captain and sailors never knew that a second slave had been their passenger. But, the Captain, hoping to set himself right with his patrons North and South, and make it safe for him to return to Virginia with his trade, went to New Bedford, and offered, through an advertisement, in a paper in that city, a reward of five hundred dollars, for the return to him of this young man, who had so dexterously eluded his grasp. But, he did not find him. He, with his fellow-traveller, was sitting by our fireside, while, with bolted doors and barred windows, we were hastily, with the help of one of our neighbors, fitting them out with warmer clothing for their wintry journey northward. We had no time for anything more than to pick up what we could find, whether it fitted them or not ; for we dared not keep them longer than was absolutely necessary. And when one of them put on a straight-collared, round-cut Quaker coat, which was much too large for him, the grotesqueness of his appearance caused them as well as ourselves, much merriment, despite the sombre aspect of the situation.

3

Our neighbors did not all sympathize with our thus setting at nought, the law of the land; which Daniel Webster, the great expounder, had so severely implored us to obey. (One pious old deacon, in the Baptist Church, said, when the story got abroad, that we had no right thus to violate the law of the land.) Had the slave-catchers come for those young men, we should not have opened our doors to them, and we should have done everything in our power, consistent with our peace principles, to prevent their capture. The consequences would, probably, have been serious to us, but we were prepared for whatever they might be, feeling sure, that we were obeying a higher and more imperative law. Our children and our servants entered heartily into our sentiments, although some of our Christian neighbors did not.

The fugitives reached Canada in safety, as the returned post-mark soon informed us; but, whether they were ever joined by their wives and children, we never learned.

Another night, good Robert Adams aroused us with a carriage full—a woman and three children. She had escaped from Maryland, some time before, with her family, and established herself at Fall

River, as a laundress; had made herself a home, and was doing well. Her eldest boy, of seventeen years, worked in a stable; and, after a while, had gone six miles away to work for a farmer. Soon after this, the same officer who arrested Anthony Burns, in Boston, arrived in Fall River, and was seen prowling around the neighborhood where colored people lived; and, especially and suspiciously, peering into the stable, where this woman's son had previously worked. Always living in fear, in this so-called "land of liberty," her excitement was extreme, when learning these facts. The friends of the slave, also, understood the good reasons there were for these fears, since the State of Massachusetts had so recently bowed to the slave-power, and, in spite of the remonstrances and entreaties of the best citizens of the State, had cruelly sent back into slavery, the man whom this miscreant had captured, for the reward it would bring him. So, they hurried this woman off, with her three children, in the darkness of night, to await, at Valley Falls, the disposal of her household effects, and the bringing of her son from the farmer's. We kept them three or four days, in hourly fear and expectation of the arrival of the

slave-catcher: our doors and windows fastened by
day as well as by night, not daring to let our neighbors know who were our guests, lest some one
should betray them. We told our children, all, at
that time, under fourteen years of age, of the fine
of one thousand dollars, and the imprisonment of
six months, that awaited us, in case the officer
should come, and we should refuse to give these
poor people up; and they heroically planned, how,
in such an event, they would take care of everything; and, especially, that they would be good,
and do just as we wished, during our absence.
The Anti-Slavery spirit pervaded our entire household, during those eventful years. In this case,
our faithful Irish servants declared, that they
would fight, before this woman and her children
should be carried into slavery: and they were
ready and willing to bear their share of the burdens
incident to the occasion. So, we waited, and kept
our secret. On the third or fourth day, the boy
arrived, with money from the good friends at Fall
River, and we sent them off, still fearing their capture on the road. The laws of the slave States,
condemned the children of a slave mother, to
follow her condition: so that, if the father was a

free man, the children were all slaves. And, as the
fathers were often white men, not seldom the slave-
owners themselves, this was a very profitable arrangement; and frequently resulted in children
being not only held as slaves, but, in their being
sold on the auction block, by their own fathers.
The beautiful quadroon girls, sold in the Southern
markets, at enormous prices, carried in their veins,
the highest and noblest blood of the aristocracy of
the Southern States; and, could their history be
written, it would tell a tale of woe and sin and
outrage,

"Which no human tongue can speak."

In the case of the family of whom I write, the
children were all boys; but, the youngest child,
only a little over two years old, had evidently been
born since the escape from slavery, and was nearly
white; and the mother seemed to think he had
more right to freedom than the others; and she said
he should never be carried into slavery. So, when
they were going off, I told her if they were caught
on the train, to give him to some kind looking person, and request him to bring him to me, and I
would keep him; and that relieved her, although,

had they been caught, it is not certain that she
could have saved him thus. My husband accompanied them a part of the way to Worcester, and
told their story to the conductor, who promised to
see that they were safely started on the Vermont
road. When he came back, he told Mr. Chace,
that the Superintendent at Worcester, said they
should be taken care of, and, if no train was going
North soon enough to secure their safety, he would
put on an extra train.

The few days which followed, were full of anx-
iety ; but the envelope came back with the Toronto
post-mark, and the man-stealers lost their prey.
We had a few more experiences with escaped slaves,
which were of less interest : but in all of them we
were surprised at the amount of intelligence and
sharp-sightedness displayed by these victims of
cruelty. And, indeed, they often appeared to have
a keener sense of the difference between right and
wrong, than we should have supposed possible
under the circumstances in which they had lived ;
and which was far superior to that of the pro-
slavery multitude, which filled the churches and
market places of New England. Of course, it was
the brightest and best who were capable of sur-

mounting all the dangers and difficulties of escape
from that terrible prison-house. I remember only
two instances, in which we were deceived by im-
posters. One of these was, when we kept, for ten
days or more, an escaped burglar, from the Auburn,
New York, State Prison, a remarkably intelligent,
gentlemanly, light-colored, handsome man, who
assumed the role of a fugitive slave, to be protected
from the officers of the law, and who was, when
they finally caught him, declared by them, to be
one of the most desperate characters in the country. He made himself very interesting and agreeable to us during his stay, by his stories of
Southern life, by his elegant manners, and especially by his great desire to learn our ideas about
right and wrong, and for improvement of himself
in all directions. He didn't do us any harm, and
we hoped we did him some good. We never re-
gretted that we had, for a short time, given him a
glimpse of a life which was not criminal.

When the Liberty party was organized in 1840,
with James G. Birney as its Presidential Candidate,
my aged father, always looking for labor in some
enterprise that promised immediate results, gave
his support to that party, while we remained firm

in the Garrisonian idea, of no participation in a
Government that sanctioned slavery.

The summer and autumn of 1856, the year of the
Fremont campaign, my parents spent with us. At
a political meeting in our village, on a warm, sul-
try evening, my father was speaking in favor of
the Anti-Slavery candidate, and, in earnest tones,
depicting the horrors of slavery and the blessings of
freedom, when, suddenly, he fainted, and fell pros-
trate on the platform. We hastened to his side,
supposing he was dying, and, I remember well,
how, in my distress, I felt great satisfaction in the
fact, that the last utterance from his lips, was the
grand word, " Liberty." I knew, if he could, he
would have chosen that. He recovered, however,
and lived several years after, to bear further testimony in the slave's behalf ; but not, like Garrison,
to see slavery abolished.

The campaign of that year, was a very exciting
one : and our children entered heartily into it :
and, when the watchwords of the parties were flying
in the air, and floating from every flagstaff, they
prepared, also, to display their several predilections.
While two of my boys, Samuel and Edward, aged
thirteen and seven years, manufactured and swung

from the top of the well-house, the stars and the stripes, with "Fremont and Freedom" in flaming letters, Arnold, aged eleven, quietly constructed his flag, all by himself, and ascending to the top of our house, swung it out upon the breeze, bearing, in brilliant color, the motto of the *Liberator*, "No Union with slave-holders." I think our little girls sympathized with all their brothers, and rejoiced in the waving of both the flags.

When John Brown attempted to free the slaves, by his attack at Harper's ferry, our family was stirred by strong emotions. On the dark day, when the grand, but mistaken old man, was hung on a Virginian gallows, a solitary strip of black drapery, on our door, reminded our neighbors, that, with us, it was a day of mourning.

When the slave-holding power ushered in the rebellion, by firing on Fort Sumter, the Abolitionists, hoping to avert the horrors of a protracted civil war, held meetings throughout New England, to arouse the North to a sense of the necessity to emancipate the slaves, as the only method by which peace could be restored. But, so blind were the masses of the people, that the pro-slavery spirit was renewedly aroused thereby, and mobs and outrages once more, assailed the truest friends of the Nation.

In our village, we had a meeting appointed for a Sunday evening, to be addressed by Henry C. Wright, one of the firmest friends of humanity, this country has ever known. A few pro-slavery politicians encouraged some "rude fellows of the baser sort," to prepare themselves to break up the meeting. Anti-Slavery friends came from Providence and Pawtucket; and, accompanied by the speaker, we all walked over to the hall; rumors of the intended disturbance having reached our ears. As we approached, we saw rough looking men standing about, and, as soon as Mr. Wright began to speak, a crowd of them entered and seated themselves. They hissed and groaned and stamped, until, after several vain attempts to make himself heard, he was compelled to give up the struggle, and, in the midst of great noise and confusion, we passed out, accompanied by the mob. We Abolitionists formed a solid phalanx around our speaker, the children among us, while we walked quietly, the distance to our house, the mob following close upon us, with yells and shouts and threats of violence, and the occasional hurling of a stone; thus proving their intention to do us harm. When we reached our gate, they halted; and, when we en-

tered the house, they dispersed, apparently wearied
with their evil work, or, perhaps, ashamed and
awed by our non-resistant attitude.

Then came another duty to the Anti-Slavery
workers. As, through all the preceding years, we
had circulated petitions to Congress, for the abolition of slavery in the District of Columbia, and the
Territories, we now began to petition the President,
Abraham Lincoln, to issue a proclamation of emancipation, as the only means of staying the tide of
bloodshed and distress, which threatened our country with destruction; and, as an act of tardy justice
to the bruised and tortured victims of our national
cruelty. His first reply to such petitions was, that
he intended to put down the rebellion. If he could
do it without abolishing slavery, he should. And
so, the war went on : millions of treasure were
wasted, young manhood bled on the battle field, and
mothers' hearts were rent and torn. And when,
after years of strife and bloodshed, the President
did finally, as a military necessity, issue the proclamation of emancipation, we rejoiced with exceeding
great joy ; and made no resistance to the honor it
gave him, as the emancipator. And, when he was
stricken down by the assassin's hand, no more

sorrowing mourners than we, wept over the sad event.

In the confusion and difficulty that followed this sudden overthrow of slavery, which threw the emancipated slaves, without any resources, upon their own responsibility, much remained to be done to save them from starvation, nakedness and homelessness. The people of the Northern States were aroused to great activity in their behalf; and a widespread sympathy and generosity were extended toward them. But, none except the long-tried Abolitionists, saw the necessity of all removal of race prejudice, and the establishment of the principle of a common humanity. The public schools of Rhode Island, had, some years before this, after a severe and protracted struggle, been opened to colored children. And yet, about the beginning of the war, a lad of rare excellence and attainments, was refused an examination for admission, by the authorities of Brown University, on account of the color of his skin. In the year 1865, while the Friends of Rhode Island, were contributing liberally and working devotedly, for the relief of the freedmen, the Yearly Meeting committee, having charge of the Friends' school, in Providence, re-

fused admission to a boy and girl, the children of
a respectable colored physician of Boston, who was
to be sent, by a philanthropic association, to look
after the welfare of the emancipated slaves in New
Orleans, and who wished to place his children in a
good school during his absence. The committee
were solicited to show their interest in the freedmen, by receiving these motherless children into
the school ; but they replied that "the time had
not yet come to take such a step ;" and our appeals fell on deaf ears.

My own convictions, long since established, were
confirmed by these and other similar experiences,
that it is not right for me to give any countenance
or support to charitable or educational institutions,
maintained exclusively for colored people. The
colored people are here, by no choice of their own
—members of our body politic ; and the sooner
they are admitted to all the privileges of citizenship, and estimated solely by their merits and
qualifications, the better for all concerned. It is a
baneful policy to undertake to support two distinct
nationalities or municipalities in one common-
wealth, or two distinct social fabrics, on any basis
except that of mental and moral fitness.

All these experiences, were an important feature
in the education of our children, which, circumstances being as they were, I would, by no means,
have had them deprived of. For, there is no better
influence, toward the building up of a strong, virtuous manhood and womanhood, than the espousal,
in early life, of some great humanitarian cause as a
foundation. By such preparation, men and women
are made ready to take up all questions which con-
cern the advancement of mankind. The slavery of
the black man is abolished. The shackles have
fallen from his limbs, and he is crowned with the
diadem of citizenship. It is too late to become an
Abolitionist now. But, in the process of over-
throwing one great wrong, there is always laid bare
some other wrong, which requires for its removal,
the same self-sacrificing spirit, the same consecra-
tion to duty, as accomplished the preceding reform.
So it has ever been.

In the progress of the Anti-Slavery movement,
experience revealed the great injustice, the detri-
ment to human welfare, of the subordinate, disfran-
chised condition of woman. Every step in that
great reform, was impeded by the inequality that
depressed and degraded her. And, these experiences were to the Abolitionists, in this, as in other

directions, a liberal education. So, when the crime
of slave-holding was overcome, they became the
leaders in the Woman Suffrage cause, their children, as a rule, following in their footsteps, in the
broader more world-wide reformation, than was the
conflict for the overthrow of slavery. For, although
we have not the chain, the lash and the auction
block, in their literal sense, to complain of, there is
enough that is unjust and degrading in the condition of women, to convince us, that the work to
which this generation of reformers is called, is of
far wider significance to the progress of all mankind, than was the Anti-Slavery struggle. Blessed
are they, who, when some great cause, "God's new
Messiah," calls to them, "Come, follow me," are
found ready to obey the Divine summons.

> "Then to side with Truth is noble,
>   When we share her wretched crust;
> Ere her cause bring fame or profit,
>   And 'tis prosperous to be just.
> Then it is the brave man chooses,
>   While the coward stands aside,
> Doubting in his abject spirit,
>   Till his Lord is crucified;
> And the multitude make virtue
>   Of the faith they have denied."

VALLEY FALLS, RHODE ISLAND.
      3rd month, 3rd, 1891.

www.ingramcontent.com/pod-product-compliance
Lightning Source LLC
Chambersburg PA
CBHW021556270326
41931CB00009B/1242